THOMAS EDISON

Richard Tames

Franklin Watts
New York • London • Sydney • Toronto

Contents

© 1990 Franklin Watts
Franklin Watts Inc.
387 Park Avenue South
New York N.Y. 10016

Phototypeset by: JB Type, Hove, East Sussex
Printed in: Belgium
Series Editor: Hazel Poole
Editor: Dee Turner
Designed by: Nick Cannan

Tames, Richard.
    Thomas Edison / Richard Tames.
        p.   cm. — (Lifetimes)
    Summary: Discusses Thomas Edison's scientific career and his
successful inventions, including the light bulb, mimeograph machine,
and ticker tape machine.
    ISBN 0-531-14004-0
    1. Edison. Thomas A. (Thomas Alva), 1847-1931—Juvenile
literature. 2. Inventors—United States—Biography—Juvenile
literature. [1. Edison, Thomas A. (Thomas Alva), 1847-1931.
2. Inventors.] I. Title. II. Series: Lifetimes (London, England)
TK140.E3T28   1990
621.3′092—dc20
[B]
[92]
                                                89-29279
                                                CIP
                                                AC

A Young Businessman

Thomas Alva Edison was one of the greatest inventors who ever lived. He was born in Milan, Ohio, on February 11, 1847. By the time he died, 84 years later, he had more than 1,000 inventions to his credit. But when he first went to school the teacher sent him home after three months, declaring him "addled" (muddle-headed). Years later, Edison remembered how his mother:

" … brought me back to school and angrily told the teacher that he didn't know what he was talking about. She was the most enthusiastic champion a boy ever had and I determined right then that I would be worthy of her, and show her that her confidence had not been misplaced."

Edison's mother had been a teacher herself and so she helped him to learn at home. By the time he was nine, he had gone beyond her and was reading what he, rather than she, considered worth knowing. This lack of formal schooling may help to explain his ignorance of mathematics at an advanced level, which he never bothered to remedy, saying:

Birthplace of genius — The Edison home in Milan, Ohio.

Edison's mother "instilled in me the love and the purpose of learning." His father beat him regularly.

"I can always hire mathematicians, but they can't hire me."

Edison's main method of learning was by experiment. He turned the cellar of his parents' house into a laboratory, lined with 200 jars of chemicals — all labeled "Poison" to keep anyone from meddling with them!

Edison's father was a businessman, always keen to try new money making ventures, and it seems that his son soon showed similar interests alongside his enthusiasm for learning. When he was twelve, Edison got a job selling newspapers on the train which ran from Port Huron, where the family then lived, to Detroit, about 62 miles (100 km) away. The journey took four hours, during which time Edison sold not only newspapers but also fruit and candy. Then he had six

hours to kill in Detroit before the return trip. These he usually spent reading in a public library. Within a few months he was making a profit of $20 a week. This he used to extend his business by setting up two stalls, one selling magazines, the other vegetables and other produce. The stalls were run by two other boys, who took a share of the profits.

Even as a small boy, Thomas Edison was a daredevil and a prankster. He was the boy who fell into a canal, who nearly got killed in a grain elevator and was publicly thrashed by his father for setting a barn on fire. Less than a year after joining the railroad, he suffered an injury which was to have lasting effect on his career and personality. He was busy selling newspapers on a station platform when he saw his train begin to pull away:

"I ran after it and caught the rear step nearly out of wind and hardly able to lift myself up ... A trainman reached and grabbed me by the ears and as he pulled me up I felt something in my ears crack and right after that I began to get deaf ..."

Edison later claimed that his poor hearing was an advantage because it helped him to concentrate by shutting out irrelevant noises, especially when he worked as a telegraph operator. He also claimed that his difficulty with hearing led him to improve the newly invented telephone and to perfect the technology of recording speech and music. Finally, he said that deafness was a great advantage in business. People didn't lie when they had to shout to be understood, and all his agreements had to be put down clearly in writing.

Undismayed by his accident, Edison soon progressed from selling newspapers to printing his own — the *Weekly Herald*, which he printed in a spare freight car on the train. He also used the freight car as a traveling laboratory. As a rising "newsman," Edison soon learned to recognize a good story when he saw one. One afternoon in April 1862, he visited the offices of the *Detroit Free Press*, where he saw a proof copy of

Smiling and selfconfident, young Edison on the eve of leaving home.

the front page, carrying sensational news of a great Civil War battle being fought at Shiloh:

"I grasped the situation at once. Here was a chance for enormous sales, if only the people along the line could know what had happened."

Edison ran to the telegraph office at the Detroit station and got the operator to contact all the main stations on the line to Port Huron, asking the stationmasters to chalk up news of the battle on the boards which usually carried the daily timetable. In return, Edison offered to keep the telegraph operator in free papers for the next six months. Then he talked the newspaper's editor into letting him have 1,000 copies of the newspaper on credit. He then set off on the train.

"At the town where our first stop was made I usually sold two papers ... Before we left I had sold a hundred or two at five cents a piece. At the next station ... (I) sold 300 papers at ten cents each."

By the time he reached Port Huron, the price had risen to 25 cents. Edison saw that there was money to be made from the telegraph, so at once he decided to become a telegraph operator.

With the Civil War raging in the United States, and both sides using the telegraph to control the movement of vast armies, there was a great demand for skilled operators. But how was Edison to learn these skills? The opportunity came in a very unusual way.

One afternoon, while the train was waiting at Mount Clemens station, Edison (who was then fifteen years old) was looking at the chickens in the stationmaster's backyard while the train's crew shunted freight cars. Suddenly, as the wagons began to roll out of the siding, Edison was horrified to see the stationmaster's two-year-old son sitting in the middle of the track. Edison hurled himself into the path of the wagons, snatched up the child and dived to safety on the far side of the track. The child's grateful father was too poor to reward him with money, but he offered to teach him how to use the telegraph. Edison was delighted to accept the offer, and within weeks was a better operator than his teacher.

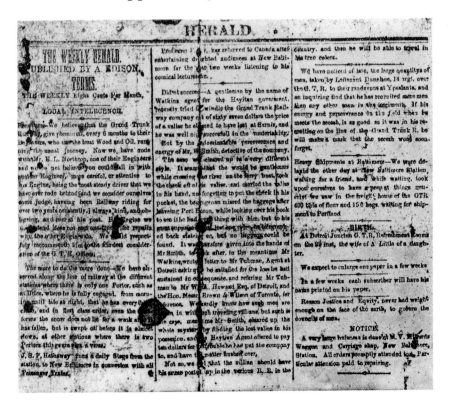

Putting his name in print. Edison's *The Weekly Herald* gave early evidence of his flair for publicity.

The Telegraph

Beginning of a great enterprise — the *Niagara* paying out the American end of the transatlantic cable which then allowed messages to be sent between the United States and Britain.

The telegraph, a device for sending messages along wires, was the first major invention in telecommunications. In 1833, two German scientists, Gauss and Weber, used copper wire to carry an electric current to a **galvanometer** — an instrument that measures electric current. By varying the current, it was possible to give different readings on the galvanometer, and so send messages.

The first public electric telegraph system was devised by Cooke and Wheatstone in England in 1838. Using electric current and a galvanometer to make five needles move and point to various letters of the alphabet, it was used to spell out information about train movements on the Great Western Railway. An American, Samuel Morse, introduced his Morse Code in the same year — a dot and dash code of long and short signals. As these were sounds, and did not involve other moving parts, messages could be sent faster than by the alphabet system. By 1844 the telegraph was widely used by the press and business world, and in 1866 it became possible to send messages between the United States and Britain via a cable under the Atlantic.

The Tramping Telegrapher

Edison soon found a job as a telegraph operator, but he didn't let a little matter like work get in the way of his education. The basement of the Port Huron telegraph office quickly became yet another Edison laboratory. For the next six years he was what was called a "tramp operator," moving from one telegraph office to another. Sometimes he chose to leave; sometimes he was sacked for paying too much attention to his experiments. He was occasionally unreliable, but when he did concentrate on his telegraphy work he was able to send and receive messages very fast.

By 1868, Edison was working in Boston as a telegraphist with Western Union. Here, he read *Experimental Researches in Electricity*, a book by the British scientist Michael Faraday. Faraday's careful description of his methods of working seemed to Edison a model of how to acquire new knowledge. After reading Faraday, he began to work much more thoroughly, concentrating on each problem until it was solved.

It was in Boston, at the workshop of Charles Williams (who was later to build Alexander Graham Bell's revolutionary invention, the telephone) that Edison made his own first invention. As a telegraphist, taking down news for the press, Edison had often copied out lists of votes on proposals put before the United States Congress. Every vote took anything up to an hour, as each congressman in turn answered to his name and called "Yea" or "Nay." Edison invented something to speed the process: simple "Yes/No" switches which could be installed beside each

London's main telegraph office, 1871.

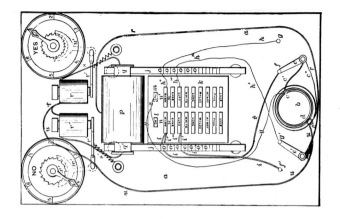

member's desk. They would be connected to the Speaker's desk, where two dials would show the total numbers of yes and no votes.

Edison paid a lawyer to take out a **patent** on his invention and then went to Washington to demonstrate it to Congress. The response was crushing:

"Young man, if there is any invention on Earth that we don't want down here, it is this."

Edison later learned that congressmen actually found the long, slow voting ritual useful because they could do deals with one another or change their minds during it, depending on how the voting was going!

Undeterred by this failure, he boldly inserted a notice in the *Telegrapher* to inform the world that he was giving up his telegraphy work and would now "devote his time to bringing out inventions."

Edison soon set up in business. He became interested in the stock ticker, an electrical machine that sent information about changing prices on the Stock Exchange to businessmen in various cities.

Edison improved the stock ticker so that it could print letters as well as figures, and opened an agency that supplied Stock Exchange information to about 40 firms, who each paid a fee for the service.

His other interest was "multiplex" telegraphy — a means of sending more than one message at a time over a single telegraph wire. If he could work out how to do this, sending telegraph messages would become cheaper.

Edison worked enthusiastically on the project and borrowed $800 to finance it. However, his experimental apparatus was a complete failure and he lost all his money. Leaving Boston in disgust, he borrowed the train fare to New York, arriving penniless.

The young inventor — an employer called him a "fiend for work."

The Age of Invention

With the crisis of the Civil War (1861–5) over, the United States entered a period of rapid economic growth. The country's immense resources and "go get it" attitude spurred people of ingenuity to find new ways of doing things. It was a period of rapid technological development, as the following inventions of just one ten-year period show.

Between 1867 and 1876, American inventors produced the first barbed wire, railroad air brakes, flat-bottomed paper bags, toilet paper, reinforced concrete buildings, cable cars, illustrated daily newspapers, riveted jeans, electric dental drills, corrugated paper and the **mimeograph**. This last — a machine for making copies of letters — was invented by Edison.

A cartoon shows self-taught Faraday, Edison's hero, using his phonograph.

"A Bloated Eastern Manufacturer"

Edison arrived in New York without a job and with nowhere to stay. He called on Franklin L. Pope, chief engineer of the Laws Gold Reporting Company, which informed traders about minute-by-minute shifts in the price of **bullion** on the Gold Exchange. Mr. Pope had no job to give, but he did allow Edison to sleep in the cellars of the Laws Company offices. Edison spent his spare time examining the transmitting equipment to find out how it worked.

One day, the transmitter suddenly broke down during trading hours. Chaos quickly followed as messengers raced in from dealers' offices, demanding to know why the system had failed. Until it was restored, they could not do business. There was a state of panic until Edison calmly announced that he knew what was wrong and could fix it. The fault was simple — a spring had broken and jammed two gear wheels. Within two hours Edison had mended the apparatus and restarted the system. Within a month, Pope resigned and Edison took his place as chief engineer at the handsome salary of $300 a month.

A few months after his resignation, Pope set up business with Edison. Between them they offered to supply every sort of electrical apparatus from specialized telegraph systems to fire alarms. Edison soon had a success on his hands with an improved "gold printer" which showed the price of gold and offered subscribers a better and cheaper service than that offered by his former employers, Western Union. Western Union met this challenge head-on by buying the rights to the new gold printer. Edison's share of the proceeds was $5,000 and a continuing stream of jobs from Western Union, researching new devices and trouble-shooting existing systems.

After a while, Western Union asked Edison how much he wanted for the rights to the various improvements he had made to the company's equipment. Edison was prepared to settle for $3,000. But, rather than name a figure, he asked Western Union to make him an offer. Their spokesman asked "How would $40,000 strike you?" Edison struggled not to gasp and then agreed it was a fair price!

Edison used the money to set up a factory in Newark, New Jersey, for making stock tickers and other office equipment. The business prospered and Edison wrote to his parents that he was in danger of becoming what they would call "a bloated Eastern manufacturer." Within a year, he decided to get married. His bride, Mary Stilwell, was just sixteen. Edison was 24. They were to have three children — Marion, Thomas and William. Edison nicknamed the first two Dot and Dash.

The Automatic Telegraph Company now asked Edison to

improve its system of automatic telegraphy. Manual telegraphy involved an operator tapping out dots and dashes onto a paper tape and then feeding it through a transmitter at speeds of some hundreds of words a minute. The theory was fine, but in practice the system often broke down or sent garbled messages.

Edison began to examine each part of the system methodically, working non-stop for days at a stretch. One of his assistants described how Edison worked:

"He ate at his desk and slept in his chair. In six weeks he had ... made 2,000 experiments on the formulas and had produced a solution — the only one in the world — that would do the very thing he wanted done." By the time he had finished, Edison had produced a system capable of transmitting 500 words per minute.

Edison soon returned to the idea of multiplex telegraphy. The result was a **"quadruplex"** which would send two messages simultaneously from each end of a wire. He sold this invention for $30,000, all of which he lost in trying to extend the system so that it would send *six* messages instead of four! Failure was, however, soon followed by triumph as Edison devised a superior receiver for Alexander Graham Bell's newly-invented telephone. He sold the patent right to Western Union for $100,000 with the curious condition that he should receive it not as a lump sum, but as $6,000 a year for 17 years. This cost him about $100,000 in lost interest that a lump sum could have earned, but his reasoning was based on a knowledge of his own weaknesses:

"My ambition was about four times too large for my business capacity and I knew that I would soon spend this money experimenting if I got it all at once, so I fixed it that I couldn't. I saved seventeen years of worry by this stroke."

Man of property. The mature businessman looking unusually composed and well-groomed. (Overleaf) **Bell and Edison telephones are compared.**

Graham Bell's first telephone.

Transmitter.

Receiver.

Instruments Exhibited at Philadelphia in 1876.

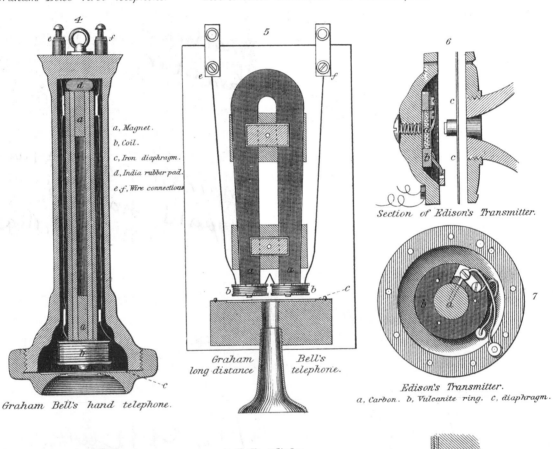

a, Magnet.
b, Coil.
c, Iron diaphragm.
d, India rubber pad.
e.f, Wire connections

Graham Bell's hand telephone.

Graham Bell's long distance telephone.

Section of Edison's Transmitter.

Edison's Transmitter.
a, Carbon. b, Vulcanite ring. c, diaphragm.

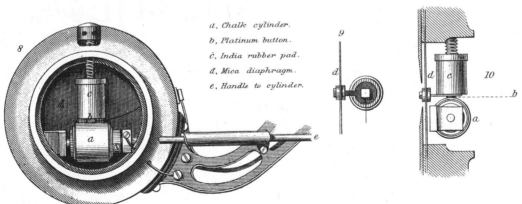

a, Chalk cylinder.
b, Platinum button.
c, India rubber pad.
d, Mica diaphragm.
e, Handle to cylinder.

The Wizard of Menlo Park

By 1876, Edison had decided he wanted to work neither as a manufacturer nor as a scientist but as an inventor who would bridge the gap between the two:

"I do not regard myself as a pure scientist ... I am only a professional inventor. My studies and experiments have been conducted entirely with the object of inventing that which will have commercial utility."

Edison wanted to get away from his Newark factory and looked for a place where he and his team of

(Right) **A rather fanciful portrait of Edison perfecting the phonograph.** (Below) **The Edison lamp works at Menlo Park, 1880.**

assistants could work without distractions and in pleasant surroundings. At Menlo Park, about 25 miles (40 km) from New York, he established his "invention factory" — a laboratory stuffed with more scientific equipment than most universities could boast at that time, plus a machine shop and a carpenter's shop and, later, a library.

If Edison wanted to work without distractions, it was not because he wanted an orderly routine. He could work for twenty hours at a stretch, or do the opposite, as one of his colleagues recalled:

"He could go to sleep anywhere, anytime, on anything. I have seen him asleep on a workbench with his arm for a pillow; in a chair with his feet on his desk; on a cot with all his clothes on. I have seen him sleep for 36 hours at a stretch, interrupted for only an hour while he consumed a large steak, potatoes and pie, and

Edison was far from easy to work with but his assistants adored him. If he made great demands on them they were no less than he made on himself as he worked to exhaustion (below).

smoked a cigar, and I have known him to go to sleep standing on his feet."

In 1877, inspired by the work he had done on improving Bell's telephone, Edison pursued the idea of not merely transmitting speech but recording it. The result was the **phonograph**, or gramophone as we now call it. This entirely original invention astonished its inventor as much as it did his sceptical assistants. In the first week of December, Edison gave a sketch of an experimental apparatus to John Kreusi, a Swiss watchmaker who was one of his longest-serving assistants. When Edison told him he was going to use it to record speech, and then have the machine talk back, Kreusi had little faith in it. However, on Thursday December 6, Edison and his team assembled in the laboratory to test the apparatus. Edison recited "Mary had a little lamb" into the **diaphragm** of the machine, while turning a handle which moved its tinfoil-covered cylinder past a needle connected to the diaphragm. When he had finished, he moved the cylinder back to its starting point, connecting it with a second needle and diaphragm arrangement on the other side of the machine. When he cranked the handle again the cylinder revolved, moving past the second needle, and out came a recording of the nursery rhyme. Even Edison was astonished!

Within a week he had shown his invention to the editor of *Scientific American* magazine:

"Mr. Thomas A. Edison recently came into this office, placed a little machine on our desk, turned a crank and the machine enquired as to our health, asked how we liked the phonograph, informed us that *it* was very well and bid us a cordial goodnight."

Edison immediately sold the phonograph idea to showmen who used it to record music, foreign languages and animal noises and then charged amazed audiences to hear these marvels played back. However, at first Edison thought the most important use of the phonograph would be as a dictating machine for use in business, not entertainment.

In fact, the phonograph marked the beginning of the recorded music business. Edison told the New York *Graphic* that the phonograph was "my baby and I expect it to grow up to be a big feller and support me in my old age." It did!

Electric Light

He had conquered sound, now Edison set out to produce electric lighting that would be cheap, safe and reliable. In theory, all that was needed was a fine fiber or wire of some sort (the filament) sealed inside an airless glass bulb. A current of electricity passing through the wire would heat it until it glowed brightly. The problem was to turn the theory into practice. What should the wire be made of? How could a vacuum be produced cheaply and easily inside a glass bulb? What size and shape should the bulb be?

Edison knew he was going to need a lot of money to pay for experiments, so he gathered a group of business backers to establish the Edison Electric Light Company. This would own all of Edison's electrical inventions, whether they were for power, lighting or heating.

It took Edison just over a year to invent a practical light bulb, confounding the sceptics who said it would be impossible to make one that would last longer than twenty minutes. One of his bulbs burned for 1,589 hours. Then came the challenge of devising a system for distributing electric power over a wide area from a central generating station. Without such a system, only those homes or businesses that could afford their own **dynamo** could have electric lighting. During 1880, Edison applied for nearly 40 patents to cover the various devices he invented for his electricity distribution system.

Meanwhile, shares in the Edison Electric Lighting Company rose from $100 each to $3,000. At Menlo Park, a long line of electric street lamps stretched through the town, to the wonder and delight of onlookers.

Edison demonstrated his new invention in Paris in 1881, at the first French Electric Exposition. He built what was then the world's largest dynamo for the purpose. The 27-ton giant could light 1,200 lamps.

The *Scientific American* magazine illustrates Edison's electric lamp for its readers. Note the wall-mount like a gas-bracket.

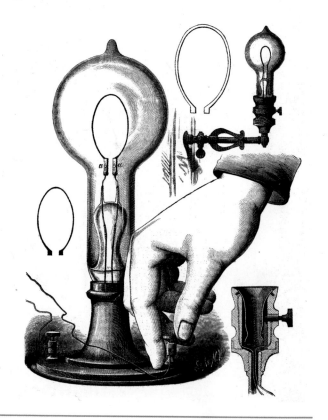

This success led to lighting companies being set up in France, Britain, Holland, Belgium and Italy. Germany followed in 1882 and Russia in 1883, when Edison lit up Moscow for the coronation of the new **Tsar**. The Paris dynamo, meanwhile, had been shipped to England, where it was installed in the world's first electricity generating station, at Holborn Viaduct in London's business

A youthful-looking Edison (left) **experimenting with carbonized paper in his search for a practical filament.** (Below) **New York's Pearl Steet generating station, 1882.**

The second Mrs. Edison — Mina Miller. Their son was to become governor of New Jersey, Edison's adopted state.

district. Later that same year, New York's first power station was opened in Pearl Street. By the end of 1883, Pearl Street was lighting 10,000 lamps for 431 customers.

A bewildering variety of institutions now clamored to install an Edison lighting system, including newspapers and theaters that needed to work by night, owners of cotton mills and color-printers, who wanted to extend the working day, and Jay Gould, a millionaire who didn't need to work at all, but wanted electric lighting for his new yacht, *Atlanta*. Edison himself was enthused about the possibilities of electricity for the ordinary family and home:

" ... it can be used to drive miniature fans for cooling purposes, to operate a sewing machine, to pump water, to work a **dumb waiter** or elevator, and for a hundred other domestic uses which now require personal labour."

In the summer of 1884, tragedy struck Edison with the sudden death of his wife from typhoid fever. For a while he drifted but then met, fell in love with, and two years later married, Mina Miller. She was a wealthy, attractive and well-educated girl almost twenty years younger than him. Unlike the first Mrs. Edison, Mina made a determined attempt to clean up her husband's scruffy appearance and control his more eccentric behavior. The newlyweds moved in 1886 to a house in West Orange, New Jersey, which was to be Edison's home for the rest of his life. Here he raised a second family — Madeleine, Charles and Theodore. Here, too, Edison built a new, larger laboratory, which he planned as the heart of a group of factories:

"My ambition is to build up a great industrial works in the Orange valley ... the laboratory supplying the perfected invention models, patterns and fitting up necessary machinery in the factory for each invention."

Over the next twenty years, Edison was to turn this dream into a reality.

The Edison Effect

Edison took pride in the fact that he was a practical inventor, rather than a theoretical scientist, but on at least one occasion his passion for the practical made him overlook an important discovery. While he was working on the development of the electric light bulb, he noticed what came to be called the "Edison effect." When a carbon filament overheated, the carbon evaporated and condensed on the inside of the bulb. Edison noticed a clear streak in the carbon deposit and figured out what the cause must be — carbon atoms were being shot in straight lines from one side of the looped filament and the other side was getting in the way of the flow of carbon, thus casting a "white shadow."

Edison investigated this curious phenomenon by putting a metal plate between the two arms of the loop. His results showed that the current surged in one direction only. He thought the experiment important enough to patent, but could see no immediate use for it. In 1897, fourteen years later, J. J. Thomson's discovery of the **electron** provided scientific confirmation of Edison's observation. This soon led to the invention of the **thermionic valve**, which in turn led to the development of radio, television and the whole modern electronics industry.

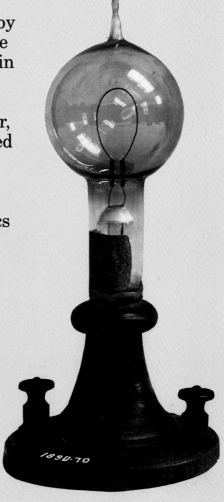

Experimental light bulbs used to test the effects of varying shapes. Edison's genius was for practical problems, rather than theoretical issues.

Edison versus Swan

Edison had an English rival for the honor of being the first to produce a commercially practical electric light. He was Joseph (later Sir Joseph) Swan, who was born in Sunderland in 1828.

Edison began his experiments with light bulbs in September 1878. Three months later, Swan announced that he had invented an electric lamp, but could offer no demonstration as his trial model had burned out during an experiment. He showed a similar lamp during a lecture at Sunderland on January 18, 1879. Meanwhile, Edison continued to work on his light bulb and, later that year, on November 1, patented it. Swan improved on Edison's filament, using a carbonized sewing thread like the one Edison had tried, but making it longer-lasting. Edison's light bulb went into production in October 1880. Swan's version was patented the following month and went into commercial production early the following year.

Man into Myth

In 1888, Edison invented an instrument "which does for the eye what the phonograph does for the ear." He called it a **"kinetoscope,"** an early form of cinema. It was basically an animated peep-show; the viewer looked through an opening and saw moving pictures of dancers, performing animals and anyone else Edison could persuade to be filmed in what was the world's first film studio. The kinetoscope could not, however, throw a moving image onto a screen, so it could not be seen by a large audience. This was not achieved until 1896. His attempts to put sound and vision together to produce **"talkies"** cost him a lot of time and money but ended in failure. Nevertheless, he was quick to see that film could be used for education as well as for entertainment:

" ... a large part of education in coming generations will not be by books but by moving pictures ... Children don't need many books when they are shown how to do things. They can learn more by some kinds of moving pictures in five minutes than they can by the usual kind of books in five hours."

Edison's main interest during the 1890s was a project to develop a method of extracting iron from low-grade **ore**. America's growing steel industry needed more raw materials every year. But high-grade ore could only be found in the far west, involving high transportation costs to bring it east to the steelworks.

From sound to light — Edison's kinetoscope (left) **and film studio** (below) **laid the groundwork for the modern cinema.**

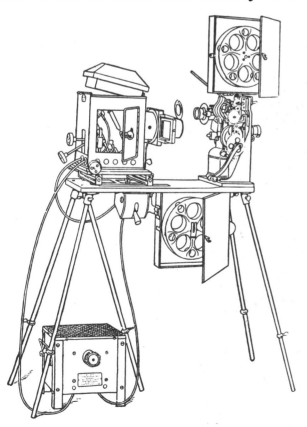

There were low-grade iron ore deposits in the east, however, and a cheap method of extracting the iron from these would be worth a fortune. Indeed, Edison spent a fortune trying to develop one, but the sudden discovery of rich iron-ore deposits in Minnesota opened up a totally unexpected source of supply for the industry. Edison's ingenious works simply couldn't compete on price and he closed them down, having lost $2 million — almost all the money he had made from his electricity business. He took it philosophically:

"Well, it's all gone," he said, "but we had a hell of a good time spending it!"

Edison also knew that hard-worn knowledge can be applied elsewhere. In 1898, rock suitable for making cement was discovered not far from West Orange. Edison bought a large area of land there and built a cement works, adapting the machinery and layout he had devised for his iron-ore works. By 1905 this new venture had become the fifth largest cement works in the United States. With his usual foresight, Edison realized that dirt tracks would soon be replaced

by smooth cement roads for wheeled vehicles. He also saw cement as an ideal cheap building material for small, new homes which would rehouse the inhabitants of the slums of America's cities.

Henry Ford (left and above)**, creator of mass-production automobile manufacture was one of Edison's warmest admirers. For a number of years, the two men went together on long trips in the American wilderness.**

Henry Ford (left) **with Edison** (third left) **and President Hoover** (right) **at Ford's Dearborn Museum in 1929.**

His next project took him back to the field he knew best — electricity. He improved the electric battery, giving it more power, making it last longer and ensuring it was less easily damaged by overcharging.

With the outbreak of World War I in 1914, the American government turned to Edison as a key adviser on defense. He wanted America to stay out of the war, but he also recognized the necessity of a strong defense. He also saw that science could make a vital contribution. When the Secretary of the Navy, Josephus Daniels, wrote to him and invited him to become president of an advisory group of scientists, Edison readily agreed. Heading a committee, however, was not a task he could take to easily. For one thing he was an individualist, used to giving orders, not working as part of a team. For another, his deafness meant that someone had to sit next to him throughout meetings, tapping out the discussion in Morse on his wrist. Edison's real contribution came through his own scientific work on torpedo-detection methods and perfecting more efficient sailing lights and **periscopes**.

By the 1920s, Edison was, quite simply, the most famous living American. Now in his 70s, he worked only sixteen hours a day! The press constantly asked his views on an incredible range of subjects. And his views were newsworthy — expressed in clear and forceful language and often remarkably perceptive, whether dealing with the possibility of harnessing nuclear energy, or the problem of traffic in great cities.

Naturally, he was showered with honors. He was elected to the American Academy of Sciences, and in 1928 Congress ordered a special gold medal to be made in his honor. But if anyone thought such gestures were going to mark the end of his active career, they were mistaken.

In 1927, the 80-year-old inventor founded the Edison Botanic Research Company to find a new way of making rubber so that America could have its own supply. After examining more than 14,000 plants, Edison decided that a variety of goldenrod offered a possible source of rubber. It did, but the process was too expensive to be a practical alternative. The onset of illness prevented him from finding a way to make it cheaper.

The fiftieth anniversary of the invention of the light bulb was celebrated in 1929. Edison's friend, the car manufacturer and industrialist Henry Ford, had set up a museum at the Ford headquarters in Dearborn, Michigan. One of its star exhibits was an exact re-creation of Edison's laboratory at Menlo Park. Edison only detected one fault: "Our floor was never as clean as that." The government also marked the occasion by issuing a special postage stamp, showing Edison's prototype light bulb.

Edison made his last public pronouncement in June 1931. The United States was in the grip of financial depression, so Edison took the opportunity to send a message of goodwill to lighting engineers meeting at a conference:

"I have seen many 'depressions' in business. Always America has come out strong and more prosperous. Be as brave as your fathers were before you. Have faith — go forward."

Edison died four months later, on October 18. Appropriately, for the man who brought electric light to America, on the day of his funeral the torch of the Statue of Liberty was extinguished as a mark of respect.

Edison kept on working to the end (above and overleaf) **and left behind 3,400 notebooks.**

The Electric Age

The first users of electric lighting were places which needed to work beyond normal daylight hours. By the year 1879, however, many other places realized they could benefit, too — art galleries, ballrooms, hotels, libraries, ocean liners and underground railroad stations. Seaside "illuminations" turned electric lights into a form of entertainment. By 1881, a coal mine, railroad carriages and shops had been added to the list. Because electricity is such a versatile form of power, many devices were invented during the second half of the nineteenth century. These are just a few: fire alarm (1852); burglar alarm (1858); dental drill (1875); miner's lamp, tramcar, advertising sign (1881); electric iron, electric fan (1882); lift, oven, sewing machine (1889); kettle, flashlight (1891); central heating, toaster (1893); electric drill (1905); toy train set (1897).

Electric railway at Menlo Park. Note the hand-operated brake.

Find Out More ...

Important Books

Edison: the man who made the future by Ronald W. Clark (Macdonald & Jane's, 1977)
Edison by Mathew Josephson (McGraw-Hill, 1959)

Thomas Edison by Josephine Ross (Hamish Hamilton, 1982)
Pioneers in Telecommunications (British Telecommunications, 1985)

Important Addresses

The Henry Ford Museum
Dearborn
Michigan
USA

Important Dates

1847 February 11, born Milan, Ohio
1854 Moves to Port Huron, Michigan
1855 Briefly attends school
1859 Becomes newsboy on Grand Trunk Railroad
1862 Learns telegraphy
1863 Becomes a "tramp" telegraph operator
1868 Moves to Boston, patents vote recorder
1869 Moves to New York, perfects stock ticker
1870 Establishes factory at Newark, New Jersey
1871 Marries Mary Stilwell
1872 Perfects automatic telegraph
1873 Invents quadruplex telegraphy
1876 Establishes "invention factory" at Menlo Park
1877 Invents phonograph and improved telephone receiver
1878 Invents electric light bulb

1882 Inaugurates New York power station and first hydroelectric plant
1883 Notes "Edison effect"
1884 Death of his first wife
1886 Marries Mina Miller and moves to West Orange
1888 Perfects improved phonograph
1889 Invents kinetoscope
1892 Embarks on major iron-ore project
1898 Begins to manufacture cement
1904 Markets an improved battery
1915 Becomes President of Navy Consulting Board
1917 Improves torpedo detection methods
1927 Begins search for alternative source of rubber
1928 Awarded Congressional Gold Medal
1931 October 18, dies

Glossary

Bullion Bars of gold or other precious metal.

Diaphragm A device that vibrates when sound hits it.

Dumb waiter A machine like a small elevator, used to send food from the kitchen to a dining room on another floor of a building.

Dynamo A machine for making electricity.

Electron An atomic particle charged with electricity.

Galvanometer A device that measures electric current.

Kinetoscope An early form of film projector.

Mimeograph An early duplicator, using a stencil, that could make copies of documents.

Ore Rock containing valuable minerals.

Patent An official document that gives an inventor the legal right to his or her invention so that nobody else can copy it.

Periscope A device enabling submarine crew to see what is happening above them at sea level.

Phonograph A machine that recorded sound and played it back. An early form of gramophone or record player.

Quadruplex A system of telegraphy that enabled four messages to be sent along a wire at the same time.

Talkies Name given to early sound films: short for "talking pictures."

Thermionic valve A vacuum tube containing a cathode and an anode, allowing electrons to flow in one direction only.

Tsar The name once given to the ruler of Russia.

Index

Picture Acknowledgements

The publishers would like to thank the following for their kind permission to reproduce their photographs in this book:
The Hulton Picture Company, 22; The Mansell Collection, cover, frontispiece, 10 (bottom), 13,15,18,19 (top), 28; Mary
Evans 9,14,16,25,26,30,31; The Wayland Picture Library, 4,5,7,8,10 (top), 11,15 (bottom), 19 (bottom), 20,21,23 (right), 24.